At The Foot Of The Cross

Lent/Easter Dramas

Dennis M. Maurer

D1445649

CSS Publishing Company, Inc., Lima, Ohio

ISBN 0-7880-1549-4

To my friends at English Lutheran Church, Bluffton, Ohio, whose gracious encouragement, and eager participation in producing these and other dramas made my own Lenten journey and my ministry among them so meaningful.
Soli Deo Gloria!

Table Of Contents

At The Empty Tomb

On The Road

Foreword

Lent is a busy time for most pastors. There are midweek services to plan, extra sermons to prepare, Easter celebrations to get organized — along with all the usual parish activities, hospitalizations, and so on. It is no wonder that so many of us find it difficult to observe Lent ourselves. The following dramatic conversations invite you to allow your parishioners the opportunity to share the Good News with you, even as you lead them in their own wrestling with the cross and the meaning of Jesus' death and resurrection for them. Imagine your own church with a large wooden cross, the nave darkened, a spotlight on one of those who were there when they crucified our Lord, pouring out his or her heart to Jesus, speaking for you, pouring *your* heart out to the Lord.

It is my prayer that this indeed might happen for you and for your congregation as together you perform these dramatic conversations. May you be blessed this Lent as you find yourself and your Lord *At The Foot Of The Cross.*

Dennis M. Maurer

At The Foot Of The Cross: Judas

"I Am The One"

Setting
Judas is standing off to the side of the cross. It is after he has betrayed Jesus and now he must face what he has done. He is distraught, upset, on the verge of a breakdown. He is talking to himself. The reader may want to use a slightly different voice for the inner Judas.

It is so *dark* tonight ... and *so cold* ...
> Oh, Judas, it's just *you* that's cold.

I know. I feel so empty inside.
> What have you done, Judas? What have you done?

What have I done? I have handed Jesus over to his enemies.
> Why would you do such a thing?

I thought I was doing him a favor.
> You were only trying to help.

Yes, Jesus kept talking about bringing in the kingdom, that God's kingdom was near — close at hand.
> You thought Jesus only needed a push, a bit of encouragement — to give the word and set the rebellion into motion.

Yes, that's it. It's Passover; Jerusalem is filled with people sick and tired of the Romans. Just one incident, just the right word even, and they would rise up in arms and make Jesus king.
> You had Jesus' best interests in mind.

I wanted to save him from himself ... Jesus, you were going soft, letting Mary waste that expensive perfume on your feet! Of all the ridiculous things — why that money could have been put to better use. It could have been given to the poor to enlist their support, or it could have been used to buy arms, or for ourselves ... And then all that talk about her anointing you for your death ... That was just crazy talk, Jesus ... the talk of someone losing his taste for the battle ahead.

So what went wrong, Judas?

What didn't go wrong? He never gave the word. He told the disciples to put their weapons away! He let them *take* him! He let the Romans and the Temple police *take him prisoner* ... Unless we do something Jesus is going to die....

That's not what you wanted ...

Oh, Jesus, why didn't you stop me? I thought you *wanted* me to go through with my plan. You seemed to know. You told me yourself, "Whatever you have to do, do it quickly" ... and so I left the supper. Jesus, sweet Jesus ... why didn't you stop me?

Maybe you are just a bit player in God's plan. Maybe everything will turn out all right yet.

No, that's impossible. Jesus is in their hands now and I'm responsible. I've done it.

But you meant him no harm. You greeted him with a kiss of friendship; surely he knew you cared about him, that you were doing this for him.

I *betrayed* him with the kiss of friendship! Oh, Jesus, sweet, sweet Jesus ... what have I done?

Get a grip. You're losing it.

But he was always *so good* to me. He trusted me! He put me in charge of the treasury. I carried our money pouch.

Maybe you took it all too seriously.

No, it was an honor. Just being *with* him was an honor, but I got to be especially close to him. At the Passover meal, I was right there beside him. John on one side, me on the other. He *trusted me.*

And you let him down.

Whatever possessed me to think that I could get him to do things *my* way? Why did I ever go to the temple authorities with my harebrained scheme? If I had just kept my mouth shut, Jesus would be free tonight. And now who knows what might happen? Jesus could end up *here*, at Golgotha, on a cross — because of *ME!*

You should tell him you're sorry.

I can't tell him "I'm sorry." What good would that do? That won't set him free ... that won't take away the humiliation I've brought upon him ... that won't ease the pain he's going to experience because of me. What good are words? And besides, I could never get near him tonight. I might *never* get near enough to tell him *ever.*

You could *do* something ... to show him you're sorry. Why not put on sack cloth and ashes? Maybe he would see you and he'd know you're sorry.

What good would that do? Jesus doesn't like showy displays of piety. He told us when we fast in repentance not to put on dismal faces to let everybody know what we're doing. He said we should wash our faces and put fresh oil on our heads and do our fasting privately. He said God would know ...

Yes, *God* knows.

God knows that I've handed his Messiah over to his enemies. God knows I've betrayed my Rabbi. God knows I deserve to die in Jesus' place.

Maybe repentance is something that happens inside, where only God can see it.

Like a new heart.

Or like turning to God, facing the music, opening yourself to God's righteous anger, trusting in his mercy and grace?

I don't know if God could forgive my sin tonight. Mine is no ordinary sin. They gave me thirty pieces of silver for my Jesus ... thirty pieces of *damned* silver — damned like me ...

You can't keep that silver.

I know I can't keep it. I'm taking it back — tonight, right now. It makes my flesh crawl just to hear it jingle in my pouch. This is blood money — I've got to take it back to the Temple authorities. I've got to go back.

Maybe you'll get to see Jesus.

I don't know if I can do that — face Jesus, I mean. I am too ashamed to face him. I couldn't stand to see the disappointment in his eyes. I've let him down. Oh, Jesus, dear, sweet Jesus ... why didn't you bring in the kingdom? What were you waiting for? What hope is there for a sinner like me?

There's one way out. You may not have to face Jesus again.

Yes, and I wouldn't have to answer to the other disciples either. Who could forgive the one who betrayed his Lord and his friend? Lord, is it I? Am I the one who should die, Jesus?

Are you the one, Judas?

Yes, *I* am the one ... I *deserve* to die ... but I have to get rid of this silver first ... I have to go back to the temple ...

You are crazy, Judas.

No, I know what I'm doing. I'll do this *my* way. I owe it to Jesus. Ooo ... it is *so dark* and *so cold* tonight ...

At The Foot Of The Cross:
Mary Magdalene

"You Made Me Okay"

Setting
Mary Magdalene sits at the foot of a large cross, preferably made of barn beams. She is talking to Jesus in her heart and we are listening in to her thoughts.

Oh, Jesus ... what have they done to you? Those nails! I can't believe it — I can't believe they would do this to *you*. You aren't a criminal. You never hurt anybody. All you did was go around helping people that everyone else had either given up on or forgotten. How could they do this to you?

If they were looking for people to vouch for you, why didn't they ask those of us who followed you, who saw what you did, who knew you firsthand? Why didn't they ask US!? Maybe we could have saved you ...

If they had asked *me* I would have told them, Jesus. I would have told them how you *changed my life*.

They say I had seven demons, Jesus. I guess I never have done anything halfway. Seven demons! Some people think I'm *still* crazy for following you around the countryside and for giving you and the disciples money to live on. They say I had seven demons and when you offered to cast them out, I asked you to cast out only six!

People can be so cruel, but I don't need to tell you that. Who am I to complain, compared to what they've done to you? If only they

13

knew, if only they could understand, if only they knew you as I know you everything could be so different.

When I first met you I was a strong-headed girl from a rough working class town on the sea of Galilee. In Magdala you either had to be tough or get stepped on. And early on, I decided that no one was going to push *me* around. I was going to take charge of my life. I was going to be in control. I wasn't the following type. Maybe that was my demons at work, I don't know. All I know is I always had to be in control.

But you know, it is a funny thing, Jesus. It seemed like the more control I tried to have, the more out of control my life became. I didn't have many real friends. Oh, there were a lot of people who knew me, and I called them friends, but I never had many people who really knew me. I guess I kept most people from getting too close. And when I would get on one of my tirades, it just drove everyone farther away.

Why is it, Jesus, that when we want to be loved and accepted, and we're hurting inside, we sometimes do the very thing that drives people away and makes it hard to love us? Why can't we just tell people that we're hurting? Why do we have to wear all these masks? Why can't we just be ourselves? Maybe it's those demons in us, Jesus.

But how did *you* know me? Why is it that you weren't put off by my self-righteous controlling ways? You seemed to know me from the first moment you laid eyes on me. I remember how you looked at me — not like other men looked at me — but with the most gentle eyes — as if you could see everything that was going on inside me *and you understood*!

You never made light of me, you never assumed the worst of me, you never made me feel like a loser. No, you accepted me and listened to me, and helped me to be the person I'd really like to be — someone who isn't always short with people, someone who helps out of a sense of joy, not obligation, who loves life instead of dreading each day's difficulties. You made me okay, Jesus.

And not just me, but all the women. I can't think of a single woman you met who wasn't moved by your acceptance and compassion. I remember one woman who had been hemorrhaging for years and years. She was unclean, no one was supposed to go near her; she wasn't allowed near the Temple. All she wanted was to touch the edge of your cloak, Jesus. And when she did — you didn't get upset or scold her — you turned and said, "Take heart, daughter; your faith has made you well." And she was! Her bleeding stopped and she was free.

And remember the woman who had been bent over and crippled by her demon for eighteen years? When you were passing by and saw her there, you called her over and said, "Woman, you are set free from your misery." And you laid your hands on her shoulders and she began to stretch and straighten until she was standing there, tall as could be, jumping up and down like a kid, praising God (Luke 13:11ff).

And then the leaders of the Synagogue started to hassle you, because you did it on the Sabbath. Jesus, the Sabbath is important, we know that. But you taught us that people, even we women, are more important than keeping the Sabbath. Jesus, you don't know how good it was to hear that.

But all that caring about the sick and the demon-possessed, all that healing and helping on the Sabbath has cost you dearly, Jesus. Why can't they understand what you have been saying? Why can't they be set free from having to have the last word? Why can't they know you as we do, Jesus?

I remember the time the scribes and Pharisees brought a woman to you who had been caught in the act of adultery. They were on their way to stone her outside the city gates. "That's the law," they said. A woman taken in adultery must be eliminated from the community.

15

But when you invited the ones without any sin to throw the first stone, they just stood there — embarrassed, I think. And then one by one they began to slink away until only you and the woman were left.

You had bent down, writing with your finger in the ground. What were you writing, Jesus? Their names and *their* sins? I've always wondered. But then when they left, you stood up and said, "Woman, where are your accusers? Has no one condemned you?" And when she said, "No one," you said, "Neither do I condemn you. Go your way, and sin no more."

You gave that woman more than a second chance, Jesus. You gave her her life. That may have been the first time anyone ever treated her as a person and someone worthy of respect. When you stood up for her, it changed her life. She really did want her life to be different after that ... and all because you made her okay.

Is it any wonder that so many of us women followed along with the rest of your disciples? You gave us hope, Jesus. You made us okay. You set us free. That's why so many of us are here, at the foot of your cross, Jesus. We don't care if the authorities recognize us or not. It doesn't matter, Jesus. All that matters is that we be here for you, just as you were always there for us when we needed someone to care about us.

And yet it hurts, Jesus. It grieves us to see you hanging there, so tortured, so fragile, so helpless. Oh, God, where are you in all this? How could someone so good be so mistreated? Why did it have to be this way, Lord? Why?

Jesus ... I don't know if you can hear me or not. I know your pain must be excruciating. But I want you to know how much I appreciate all you've done for me. I will never forget you ... and I won't let the others forget either. I love you, Jesus.

At The Foot Of The Cross:
Simon Of Cyrene

"Forgive Them? Never!"

Setting
Simon of Cyrene sits at the foot of a large cross, preferably made of barn beams. He is talking to Jesus in his heart and we are listening in to his thoughts as he wrestles with his anger and personal embarrassment for being forced to carry Jesus' cross.

Well, here I am, Jesus ... back again. I got halfway to the city gate, and I turned and saw you hanging here — and I don't know what happened. I just knew I had to come back.

Why are you hanging here, Jesus? What did you do to deserve this? Nothing! At least nothing I am aware of. It's these despicable Romans. I mean, all I wanted to do was come to Jerusalem for the Passover. I saved for years for this trip. And I get here to Jerusalem and what do I find? The place is crawling with Roman soldiers. You'd think they wanted to become Jews! What are they doing here during this holy festival?

Oh, yes. I know. They're here to keep the peace. To keep us oppressed is more like it. I know these Romans, Jesus. I know what they're like. I'm from Cyrene in North Africa. We were a free city once. And then came Alexander the Great, then the Ptolemies, and then the Romans — and it was the Romans who took away our charter and made us their colony.

And thirty years or so after the Romans took over Cyrene, they entered Jerusalem, the Holy City. Sorry, Jesus. I'm still upset. You see, I never thought much about the Romans. They were there, and we would rather be free, but they kept to their business and I kept to mine and everyone was happy. At least I was at peace.

But then I come to Jerusalem! I had heard about you, Jesus, from fellow travelers on the road. People said you had worked miracles, Jesus. They said you had given sight to a man who had been born blind. Born blind! I've heard of other so-called miracle workers who gave people back some sight — but never one with the power to make a man born blind see!

And people said you did other miraculous things — like feeding a multitude — some said 5,000 men — with just a few loaves of bread and a couple of fish. Now that, I said to myself, was either a gross exaggeration, or this Jesus was someone special. Someone I wanted to meet.

I met other people though who said you were a troublemaker. Someone out to change the law of Moses. They said the scribes and the Pharisees, who know everything there is to know about the law, were out to prove that you are a heretic.

And then these past few days the whole city has been stirred up. Some people are angry with you for not being the Messiah. They feel betrayed because you didn't start the rebellion they hoped for. Others are just despondent — let down and disappointed because you aren't who they thought you are.

As for me, Jesus, I don't know what to think. I don't even know why I came back here. But I had to see you again. That's how I got into this fix this morning anyway ... I wanted to see you. But I heard this morning that you had been arrested during the night, and that you had been questioned by the Sanhedrin and then by the Romans. I thought my chances of seeing you were gone.

But then I heard all the commotion in the street and I went out and there you were ... coming along the way, struggling with the weight of the cross, stumbling.

I pushed my way closer to the front of the crowd lining the way ... and as you drew near to where I was standing you stumbled again. The Roman guards were ridiculing you, making fun of us sissy Jews. And then you looked up at me. I will never forget your face, Jesus ... your tired, pained, tragic face that seemed somehow at peace too.

No, it couldn't have been peace. It must have been resignation. I don't know ... but you had a powerful effect on me. And then it happened. The guard looked as if he had had enough. Time was wasting and the Sabbath was approaching and this execution had to be a quick one. And so he tapped me on the shoulder with his spear!

He might as well have shoved it through my chest — the effect would have been the same! For I knew what it meant to have him tap me on the shoulder. He wanted me to take up your cross and follow you.

The very idea! I am a visitor to Jerusalem. I am on a pilgrimage. I am a Jew from the important city of Cyrene. I am no country bumpkin that they can push around.

And yet, if I resisted they would have put that sword through me. And then what would become of my sons, Rufus and Alexander? I am a proud man, Jesus. Perhaps too proud sometimes. But I love my sons, and so for them, I bent down, took up your cross and followed you ... burning with anger every step of the way.

If I had just minded my own business and gone to the Temple this morning as I had planned, none of this would have happened. No, I had to see Jesus. I had to push my way to the front of the line. I had to get a good look. I am so angry I could ... I could ...

What's that? What did you say? Father ... what? Father, forgive them for they don't know what they're doing? Forgive them? Jesus, how can you say that? After all they've done to you? Forgive who?

19

These Romans who have nailed you to this cross? I mean, they could have tied you up — but no, they went all the way with nails. The pain must be horrendous. How can you forgive them?

I know I can't. I'll never forgive this lot for what they've done to me. Why, they have humiliated me as a Jew and as a man. What will my sons think of me after this? How could I possibly forgive these Romans? They are the enemies of God's people. I will never forgive them. Never! (*Pause*)

Father, forgive them for they know not what they do. Who are you, Jesus? What kind of a man are you to go through all you've endured in the past twelve hours and still want to forgive your tormentors? In all the pain you must be experiencing, how can you even *think* of others, let alone want to forgive them? (*Pause*)

Father, forgive them. Jesus, your suffering makes my embarrassment seem like nothing. I'm not the one hanging on the cross. I'm not the one falsely accused, mistreated, and abused. I'm not the one being jeered and laughed at. And yet you want to forgive them.

Why is it I feel like you are including me in that prayer? It's true, isn't it, Jesus? You're praying for me ... for my being so filled with hatred at the Romans. Is that it, Jesus? People said your preaching was different — that you said we should love our enemies, and forgive those who hate us, even if it took seventy times or more to get through to them.

Is that what this is all about, Jesus? Father, forgive them. (*Pause*) I don't know who you are, Jesus ... but go ahead ... pray for me.

At The Foot Of The Cross:
The Centurion

"I Hate Executions"

Setting

The Centurion is standing at the foot of Jesus' cross. To him this is just another execution. He is bored and talks to himself. Yet intrigued by this Jesus, he finds himself talking to Jesus too.

I hate executions. I have been in the service of Rome for thirty years now. I have been stationed in pagan Gaul and Cyrene in North Africa. I've lived in the bawdy city of Corinth and in Syrian Damascus. Over the years I have seen a lot of executions in a lot of lands and I have *never* liked them.

I'm just doing my job. But I don't much care for this part of it at all. I know, I know ... the enemies of Rome must be silenced and the crowds must be controlled — and I am as loyal as the next soldier. But I still don't like it. It brings out the worst in people. Look! (*Pointing*) My *own* men, gambling for dying men's clothes! And the crowds! Gawking, mocking, wagging their tongues. I hate the whole business.

And it is a *grisly* business too. Of course I don't have to tell you that, do I, Jesus? Flog the prisoner silly, make him carry the burden of his destruction, give the crowds a chance to taunt him, nail him to the cross, hoist him up until it thuds into its socket in the rock, making every wound scream with pain, and then wait for the victim to suffocate. What a way to die!

I know all the theories. If we make a big enough display with enough gruesome horror to it, then the average man will think twice about

21

interfering with Rome's plans and goals. Maybe it's true — the average man *will* think twice about dying like this. But what about the *unaverage* man — the above average man, the real threat to Rome? What about someone like *you*, Jesus? Fear of embracing this cross didn't deter you, did it?

Of course, you Jews are different. You cling to your God with such loyalty and tenacity. Is that what gives you strength, Jesus? Your God? Do you think your God will save you — from this? Or have you given up? (*Pause*) Why are you so quiet, Jesus? Does your God give you that much peace that you can go without even cursing us Romans from the cross?

Sometimes I envy you Jews ... and your God. We Romans have gods like Bacchus, the god of drinking and partying, revelry and merrymaking. And we have Mars, the god of warfare and soldiering. Jupiter, father of the gods, and strange gods from the east like Isis and Osiris, and Cybele [*sib 'lee*], the Great Mother.

We have gods coming out our ears! Oh yes, and we have Fate, that cruel goddess who takes our future from our own hands and makes it hers. Fate, the tyrant — sending us to early graves, keeping us from really living, making us slaves to fear and depression, victimizing a person more often than blessing one.

These Roman gods are a sorry lot, Jesus. They are as nasty and as crazy as the people who worship them. The temple dramas tell the story of their craftiness and scheming among themselves — while our lives lie in the balance. They are no comfort — not really. They are just like us — cruel, self-indulgent, lawless, demanding tyrants.

That's why so many of us stationed here in Palestine are intrigued by you Jews and your God. True, you Jews are an inflexible lot, not very tolerant of others and their gods, totally absorbed in your religion. We find that hard to take. But your devotion to him, and your fierce loyalty to this law of yours, and this Temple that doesn't

22

even have a statue of your god. How can you worship a god you cannot see?

And yet it is precisely this God of yours that makes us stop and think. You Jews claim your God is the god of history and you have a book that tells of the sins of your people and the generosity of your God who has helped you since you first became a people. All we Romans have are the stories of the gods clowning around and fighting with each other.

Your God, you say, gave you a law code — ten commandments — to guide you in the way you ought to live. Your God is a god of principles and morals — in a world of licentiousness and orgies, where people act like animals and anything goes — as long as it doesn't threaten the Empire.

But a God who cares about widows and orphans, who gives you a day off each week to rest and to hear his word, a God who forbids you to lie or steal, murder or mess around with other women or men. This is a different kind of God! Why does he care about people — even us foreigners? That's the question none of us can figure out.

Our gods seem to thrive on chaos — they create enough of it. But your book says that your God is a god of order. Our gods are vindictive and demanding, wanting prayers and offerings before they will grant our petitions — yet yours welcomes your prayers and is ready to forgive your sins. There is a graciousness about this God of yours that appeals to me, Jesus.

And not just to me. I know of others — even in the military — who have become followers of this God of yours. One of them you know — Publicus Secundus, one of the centurions stationed in Capernaum. He says you healed his servant. He's taken an interest in the God of the Jews. Why, he even helped the people there enlarge their synagogue.

And then there is my friend, Cornelius. He's stationed at Caesarea on the coast. Now there is a cushy assignment — except when dignitaries from Rome arrive. Then you have to shepherd them around like a mother hen, taking care to make them feel at home — even if we are in the middle of nowhere here in the provinces. Anyway, Cornelius is a centurion and he too has become a "god-fearer" as you Jews call us. I heard his whole family has begun giving alms to poor Jews ... they've even given up pork! Can you believe it?

Most of his fellow centurions think he has "gone native." It happens sometimes when a soldier is far from home, and everything is so new, and the local people seem to have so much more peace and harmony in their lives than you do in yours. But I think it is different with Cornelius and the other god-fearers. There is just something different about your God and his concern for ordinary people — even ordinary centurions ...

It is a very confusing world today, Jesus. Everything seems to be in a state of flux; nobody knows what to believe anymore. There are too many gods, too many choices. Nobody knows what is right or wrong. (*Pause, thinking*) The only thing that is certain is that we are going to die. Is there a god, Jesus? What is he like? Is he the God of the Jews? Does he care about the rest of us? Does he care about *me*?

And how do you fit into all this, Jesus? The placard on the cross says, "Jesus of Nazareth, Rex Iudaeorum, King of the Jews." Are you their king, Jesus? Are you the Messiah of God everyone has been waiting for? Are we right to execute you for attempting to hinder the administration of the *Pax Romana*, Rome's Peace?

Or are you something else? You are unlike anyone I have ever known or heard of. You say you were sent by your God and a lot of people think you are a holy man — and yet you were willing to go to a Roman centurion's home to heal his servant. No Jew, except collaborators, will go to the home of a Roman. And when the centurion said, "No, just say the word and my servant will be healed," you praised his faith! — and his servant recovered.

What kind of a man are you, Jesus? I'd wager that I've witnessed a thousand of these executions. I've presided over hundreds more. But I have never seen a criminal forgive his executioners before. Nor have I ever heard one make arrangements for his mother from the cross.

I have looked into the eyes of a lot of soon-to-be dead men, too, and I have never seen anyone look as tormented and yet as at peace as you do. You promised that same peace to this other character — a thief — someone who deserves to die. And yet you cry out something about God forsaking you?

Who are you, Jesus? They say you are a criminal, but from what I have seen you seem to care and act just about as your God would, if he were here. (*A great **terrifying** shout from offstage: **Aaaaugh!***) Jesus? Jesus?

(*Centurion turns from the cross to the congregation, shouting at them*) Leave him alone! Stop mocking him! Can't you see it's finished? Can't you see? (*His voice changes, trails off. Centurion turns back to Jesus*) What an unusual way to die. Most of those crucified simply moan their way into death's embrace. That awesome cry was more like the victory shout that we soldiers cry in battle. Who are you, Jesus?

(*Speaking to himself*) Could it be true? What else could it mean? Certainly, he was as godly a man as I've ever seen die. (*Pause*) Surely this man was God's son.

At The Foot Of The Cross: John

"What's Love Got To Do With This?"

Setting
John is standing at the foot of Jesus' cross. He is wrestling with the "whys" of Jesus' execution and death. He believes Jesus is the Messiah, God's Son, and yet he cannot comprehend how this fits with the cross. John remembers many things Jesus did and how Jesus changed his own life.

(*Loud whisper*) Jesus ... Jesus ... It's me, John. I've come with your mother, and some others. Don't try to say anything. I just wanted you to know that you are not alone. *Some* of us are here. We couldn't abandon you, not after all you've done for us.

I can't believe this is happening, Jesus. Everything happened so fast last night. The supper was barely over and we were in the garden and you were praying and then the soldiers came and then the back and forth between Pilate and the rest — and now *this*.

Jesus, I don't know why all this has happened, but I believe you are the promised Messiah. I believe you are God's Son. I always have, Jesus. Ever since John the Baptist pointed you out to Andrew and me, I have believed that you are the one all of us have been waiting for.

And yet that is what makes this cross so difficult to understand, Jesus. It seems like ages ago, but just a few days ago, when we entered Jerusalem, you said that you would draw everyone to you when you are lifted up from the earth. I heard you like all the rest, but I never thought it would mean the *cross*.

The crowd replied that the law says the Messiah will remain forever. How can it be that the Son of Man must be *lifted up*? That's our problem, Jesus. How does this cross fit in? How can this awful suffering, this cruel cross, draw people to you if you are dead?

And yet that is just like you, Jesus. It's one of the reasons why I am attracted to you and your gospel, for you turn all my thinking upside down. I always thought of God as *the Almighty* — far away, but you taught us to call him *"Father."* I thought getting right with God meant doing good deeds for extra credit, but you said doing God's will is simply believing in the One he sent.

I thought life with God was something that would come only at the last day, but you said it is ours now, *today* — when we trust in God's promises you shared with us. I thought the Messiah would remain forever, but you seemed almost to welcome this cross. Jesus, your thinking is so ... *different.*

You seem to know God's mind. You are like the greatest of all the prophets, and yet you are more than just a prophet. You speak and it is as if God himself were speaking. It is as if you were God's word himself come to us. That's why I have followed you, Jesus. You make God *real* to me — you help me to see God with new eyes and new understanding.

But it is not just what you've said; it is all you have *done* too. From the first sign you did at Cana to the last one at Bethany when you raised Lazarus — you made things *different* ... you made people *better* ... you brought people *life!*

I remember that wedding at Cana. The steward of the wedding feast told your mother that he was out of wine. What an awkward and embarrassing moment for the wedding couple, and what a way to start a marriage! Mary spoke to you, and a little later you sent the servants to the huge water jars, only to find them filled with wine! *Wine!* You have always had a way of taking the ordinary and making it *special.*

But the most wondrous thing you ever did involved our friend Lazarus. How many days had he been dead? Four? Mary and Martha were beside themselves with grief; we couldn't understand why you would want to re-enter Herod's territory and face certain arrest — but off we went and in the midst of all our confusion and grief you called Lazarus out from the tomb ... a *dead man!* ... and yet step by struggling step there he appeared in the doorway ... *alive!*

Jesus, wherever you went, you brought life out of death, and hope out of despair — the way things would be if God were to bring in his kingdom and make everything new. In your words and in your deeds, God and his love and power are easier to grasp. That too is why I believe you are more than a prophet, Jesus.

But the real reason I know you are the Messiah, God's Son, is that you have done all these things for *me too*, Jesus. You changed me ... made me better ... gave me life.

I used to be a hothead like my brother, James. You had our number from the very beginning. I remember you laughed at our outbursts and called us "Sons of Thunder"! It wasn't a put down, just an observation — and you were right! We *were* "Sons of Thunder"!

I remember the time we passed through a Samaritan village and none of them would believe your message. James and I were furious; we wanted to call down fire and brimstone on that village. But you rebuked us, and rightly so. Then there was the time we found someone casting out demons in your name. He wasn't one of us; he was just *using* you and we wanted to stop him. But you said not to stop him, "... for whoever is not against you is for you."

You showed me what love and acceptance are all about, Jesus — partly by loving and accepting all these people who riled me up, but also by loving and accepting *me* — *in spite of* my outbursts.

I can't believe how self-centered I have been. James and I even had the nerve to ask you to let us sit at your right and your left when you established your kingdom! If I had been you, I would have thrown us out. Instead you put on a towel, like a servant, and washed our feet. You! Our Rabbi!

I am ashamed, and yet moved, because you *never* rejected us — no matter how crazy we acted or how numbskulled we were. You loved me and the others ... and you taught me how to love — how to let go of my pride and anger, self-centeredness and conceit. I never felt like I had to impress you, Jesus. But being around you I always wanted to be better — more like *you*. Your love is a different kind of love than what I'm used to, Jesus. It must be what God's love is like.

I remember you saying something about love once. "As the Father has loved me, so I have loved you; abide in my love." And then what did you say? "I have said these things to you so that my joy may be in you, and that your joy may be complete. Love one another as I have loved you. No one has greater love than this, to lay down one's life for one's friends."

But what has love got to do with *this*, Jesus? *This cross?* It seems like the enemies of God have won. Are you saying you are laying down your life for *ours* on this cross? *Out of love?* Jesus, knowing you and your love *has* made my joy complete ... but *this cross* gives me nothing but grief. I can't understand this.

Yet I remember the first time I ever saw you. I was with John the Baptist and John pointed you out and called you God's lamb. He said you were the "... lamb of God that takes away the sin of the world." Are you God's *lamb*, Jesus?

It is Passover. Are you the Passover lamb whose blood saves us from certain death? Or are you the scapegoat, driven outside the city walls bearing all our sins? Isaiah said God would send his servant who would go like a lamb to the slaughter and by his stripes we would be healed. Are you that lamb, Jesus? Or are you the lamb of God that took Isaac's place when God commanded Abraham to offer up his only son of promise? Which lamb are you, Jesus? Or are you all of these?

Is that what this death is all about? You seemed to welcome this cross. We would have fought for you, you know. All you would have had to do was give the crowds the word and we all would have fought for you — and yet you didn't. When the people waved their palm branches and welcomed you as the Messiah, you didn't give the word then either. Instead, you started talking about *dying*, about how a grain of wheat must be buried in the ground before new grains can come to life.

My mind is reeling with memories, Jesus. I can't make sense of it all, but I am wrestling with this, Jesus. Help me. Help me make sense of your dying. Help me to accept this. I saw Lazarus with my *own* eyes. I believe you *are* the way and the truth and the life — so how does this all hang together, Jesus? Why the cross? Why this death that says everything I believe is mistaken?

Was John the Baptist *right*? Are you the lamb that takes away the sin of the world? How? How can this be? Why should someone so loving and so good have to die? And yet I believe *you would* give yourself to die in my place, Jesus. I *know* you would. Is *that* what love has to do with this? Do you love me *that much*? Are you dying for *me*, Jesus?

At The Foot Of The Cross:
Mary

"Hanging On To Faith"

Setting
Mary sits at the foot of Jesus' cross. She is heartbroken and in great pain for her son. She remembers what the angel told her and how Jesus has grown up before her eyes and how proud she is of him.

Oh, my son. How could they do this to you? Your hands ... your feet ... *even a crown of thorns!* How could they be so cruel? O Jesus ... my dear, sweet Jesus. If I could just hold you in my arms again, like I did the night you were born. If only I could get close enough just to touch you ... to let you know I'm still here and that I'd give anything to make this all go away.

It breaks my heart to see you hanging here. The others didn't want me to come, but I don't care what the guards, or your brothers, or the disciples say. I *need* to be here, Jesus. John and I and the rest of the women — we couldn't abandon you. But how it grieves me to see you in such pain. How I wish I could have saved you from this, Jesus. Maybe I wasn't the mother I could have been. Maybe I could have prevented all this suffering and agony.

What was that? What are you trying to say, Jesus? "Woman, here is your son?" John? My son? What are you saying, Jesus? You want me to look after John as my son? What? "John, here is your mother?" You want John to treat me as his mother, too: To take me into his home, to look after me? But, Jesus, I don't want anyone else to take care of me. I have always looked to you.

33

This is so strange ... and yet this is just like you. No matter how tired you were, you were always willing to make time for others, healing their sick, forgiving their sins, asking them questions that helped them to see that God is close by and cares for them. And here you are, in pain and agony, and you are still giving, still caring about others. Okay, Jesus. I will go with John. But only for you.

You have always been so good, Jesus. (*Pause*) I remember that terrifying night when I saw the angel and he promised that I would have a son and that all this would come about through the power of the Holy Spirit. I knew then you were different, special, holy. The angel said you would be called "the Son of the Most High" and that the Lord would give you the throne of your father David.

I often wondered exactly what it all meant. Isn't every child a gift from God, the work of the Holy Spirit? Aren't we all sons and daughters of God? But as you grew I knew that you *were* different from the other children. You had a different way of treating others; you were strong, yet gentle; firm, yet kind; "with us" yet beyond us somehow.

I was as happy and proud as a mother could be — dreaming about what you might become someday, and what you might do with your life, and how God might use you to bring peace and hope to our people. I remember going to see Cousin Elizabeth before you were born, and as we shared our stories, I just had to sing:

> *My soul magnifies the Lord,*
> *and my spirit rejoices in God my Savior,*
> *for he has looked with favor on the lowliness of his servant.*
> *Surely, from now on all generations will call me blessed;*
> *for the Mighty One has done great things for me,*
> *and holy is his name.*
> *His mercy is for those who fear him*
> *from generation to generation.*
> *He has shown strength with his arm;*
> *he has scattered the proud in the thoughts of their hearts.*

He has brought down the powerful from their thrones,
and lifted up the lowly;
he has filled the hungry with good things,
and sent the rich away empty.
He has helped his servant Israel,
in remembrance of his mercy,
according to the promise he made to our ancestors,
to Abraham and to his descendants forever.

— Luke 1:46-55

I was so happy because I believed God would use you to help his people, Jesus. I kept the angel's words in my heart and more than once I have gone there to wrap myself in his promise, to help me get through the day.

For besides my joy, there have also been moments when my heart would break for you, Jesus. It is just like Simeon said it would be. Joseph and I were taking you to the Temple for your dedication and circumcision. On the Temple steps we met old Simeon. He looked at you and said, "This child is destined for the falling and the rising of many in Israel, and to be a sign that will be opposed so that the inner thoughts of many will be revealed." I had no idea what his words would mean. How could I ever have known it would mean *this*?

And then old Simeon said something else that has haunted me ever since. Turning to me, he said, "... and a sword will pierce your own soul too." I still get the shivers when I think of those words. How many times did I think his prophecy had already come true? I remember the night we heard that Herod was sending soldiers to find the newborn Messiah. We were told to flee for our lives, and so I bundled you up, held you close to my breast, and we fled for Egypt.

I felt then as if my heart would break — afraid to leave our home, terrified something might happen to you, my son. Then later we heard that soldiers had come into the village. They beat down doors, tore babies from their mothers' arms, pierced their little chests with their cruel swords, and trampled their lifeless bodies under their horses' hooves. How could anyone be so cruel, Jesus? My heart ached for those mothers and for those lost sons.

Once we left you behind in Jerusalem, and I thought I had lost you forever. We assumed you were with family, and when I asked around and discovered you were missing. I felt that sword of Simeon's yet again. We rushed back to Jerusalem, asked here and there, stopping people in the streets, asking if they had seen you. And then at last, we found you in the Temple, discussing theology with the Scribes. I had been so worried, but now everything was okay, because you were okay.

I remember another time though, when things weren't okay. You had come back to Nazareth, sometime after you were baptized by John. And you helped with the worship in the synagogue and everyone was amazed at what you said and with the authority with which you spoke. But they also put you down, saying, "Where did this man get this wisdom and these deeds of power? Is not this the carpenter's son? Is not his mother called Mary? And are not his brothers James and Joseph and Simon and Judas? And are not all his sisters with us? Where then did this man get all this?" (Matthew 13:54-56).

They took offense at you, Jesus. And my heart ached for you. You only wanted the best for them, you only wanted to help, but they wouldn't let you. And then you said, "Prophets are not without honor except in their own country and in their own house." And that hurt most of all, because it was true — and not one of your brothers believed in you. They still don't. That's why I am here, all alone, except for the other women, and John.

But now it's come to *this*. All those other other times were hard, Jesus, but nothing compared to this. It is hard to accept this, Jesus. I don't understand how this cross fits into God's plan. It is hard to hang on and believe that everything will be okay, when your son is hanging here, nailed to a cross ... and everyone is saying behind your back that your faith is misplaced.

Is my faith misplaced, Jesus? I find this so hard to accept. It hurts so bad. And yet ... I still believe the angel's promise. I believe what you said, my son. And I believe that what you have done has been God's will. Even though this cross shouts, "No!" to everything I believe, this just *can't* be the end. It just can't be. Surely God must be at work here somehow. Tell me that God can bring some good out of this, Jesus. Don't let this be the end.

What? (*Looking offstage*) He says he's thirsty. Can't you give him something? What? No water? What's in that jar there? Can't we give him some of that, at least? Jesus, I'm sorry ... this is all there is ... and it's sour.

All right, Jesus. I will go with John, just as you said. And I will be okay, because I know God has done great things through you. And even though I don't understand all this I know you are in God's hands — where you have always been. But I still believe you don't deserve this — for all you've ever done was to give people *life!* (*Pause*) The angel was right, my son. You are the Son of the Most High ... but you will always be my son too, Jesus. I love you.

(*Mary shouts out Jesus' last word, then cries out*) Finished? Aaaaugh! (*She collapses with her head on her arms, sobbing*)

Maundy Thursday
Mark 14:12-26

At The Foot Of The Cross: Peter

"I'm No Rock!"

Setting
Peter sits a bit to the side, away from the cross, as though in hiding (which he is). He is wrestling with his fear and denial in contrast to Jesus' calling him Peter, or "Rock." This can be a powerful monologue on confession and experiencing forgiveness. Through Peter's reflection we come to understand that Jesus doesn't just see us as we are, but also as we might become through his love and grace.

How could I have done it? How could I have been so stupid? You told me I would deny you, Jesus, but I was so sure of myself. I just knew I would never let you down. But you knew all along, didn't you, Jesus? You said that before the rooster crowed last night, I would deny you three times. How could you know that?

I was okay. I followed you to the High Priest's house, but as I stood outside warming myself by the fire in the courtyard, they started asking me if I was one of your disciples. I was scared, Jesus. I didn't want you to get out of my sight; I didn't want to abandon you. I was afraid they would arrest me too and we would be separated.

And ... well ... yes ... I was afraid for *myself* too. I was afraid the authorities would arrest and torture me too. That's why I can't go to Golgotha; that's why I can't be there with you now, Jesus. I am afraid — we all are. We don't know what will happen next. I am so sorry, Jesus, so ashamed.

But there is another reason too, Jesus. I can't go to Golgotha because I can't bear to see what they have done to you. I can't bear to see you fastened to that cross — with the mobs mocking you, and the soldiers "doing their duty" ... ugh ... Oh, Jesus.

You gave me the name "Peter." I would have been content to have always been known as "Simon" — simply Simon. But you had to call me "Rock"! But *I'm no rock*, Jesus. I am an embarrassment — *even to myself.* I have let you down. And not just last night and today. I have let you down again and again.

I have always been impulsive. I remember that night we were out in my boat. It was so dark, and so late. We thought we were seeing some kind of ghost coming to us, walking on the water. And then we heard your voice. And I wasn't sure. I asked you to invite me out on the water too. And when you said, "Come!" I jumped right in and *I did it! I walked on the water too!*

And then I noticed the waves ... and the wind ... and I realized that I had no business being out there on the water ... and I began to sink like a rock! I thought I was going to die ... right there and then. If I'm a rock, then I'm a *sinking* rock! But I'm no rock of faith, Jesus. All I could do was cry out to you, "Lord, save me!" And you *did!*

It seems like I have always been putting my foot into things, and you had to save me. Once you told me to let down my nets when we had been fishing all night. I was tired. I told you it would do no good. But then, for you, I let them down and we took in such a catch! We had to call James and John to come with their boat to help us land the nets.

All I could do was throw myself at your feet and say, "Depart from me, Lord, for I am a sinful man." But you *didn't. You stood by me* ... in spite of all the dumb things I've done and said. After all, I was the one who asked that stupid question about how many times a

40

person ought to forgive someone. And I was the one who was "fishing" to find out what kind of a reward we would get for leaving everything behind and following you. And still you called me "Rock"!

But all that was nothing compared to last night. If only I could have that one night to live over. Everything started out so well. You sent John and me ahead to prepare for the Passover meal. And we found everything just as you had said — the man with the water jug and everything.

And then at the meal, everything seemed so sad ... like this would be our last meal together. Then you said those words that cut right through our hearts — sharper than any two-edged sword. "One of you is going to betray me...." No wonder you seemed so downcast. And all we could say was, "Lord, is it I?" instead of thinking about *you* and what you must have been going through.

You said you had to go somewhere ... there was something you had to do. And I said I would go with you. I can still hear my voice: "Lord, why can I not follow you now? I will lay down my life for you." And that's when you said to me, "Will you lay down your life for me? Very truly, I tell you, before the cock crows, you will have denied me three times." That hurt, Jesus. I just *knew* I would stand by you.

And then you took the bread and blessed it ... and broke it ... and said, "Take and eat ... this is my body." The words made my flesh crawl, Jesus. I was afraid you were telling us that *this* was the hour you had talked about so much and we had always resisted. Your body ... broken like this bread? No ... say it isn't so, Jesus.

And then when the meal was over, you took the cup of blessing — the last cup of the meal — and then *we all knew!* What did you say? "This is my blood of the new covenant, which is poured out for many...." The New Covenant — the one promised by Jeremiah? Sealed with your blood? But how? Why now? This just *can't be.*

41

But before we could take all this in, we were on our way to the garden of Gethsemane, and then Judas came with the soldiers and you were taken, and I followed and everything you said about me came true. Maybe the words of my denial were *true,* Jesus. Maybe I'm *not* one of your disciples. I don't *deserve* to be called a disciple — let alone "Rock"!

And yet *you chose me.* You called me from my fishing and you said you would make me a fisher of everyday folk. Why did you call *me,* Jesus? And why did you call me "Rock"? Was it just a joke — because you knew I would always let you down? But that's not like you, Jesus.

You seemed to *believe* in me. Not just because of my stature, or my fishing business ... but you seemed to see something in me that I can't always see — especially now. But you trusted me ... counted on me. You included me in all those special times in your life — like that night on the mountain when Elijah and Moses appeared with you ... or like the time you raised Jairus' daughter ... or like last night, when you prayed so hard in the garden. You always asked me to be there with you and James and John.

Is that the answer, Jesus? Did you call me "Rock" not because of what I *am,* but because of what I might *become*? Is that why you called me? Is that why you took me with you? So that I might *become a rock*?

What was it you said to me, Jesus? "Satan has demanded to sift all of you like wheat, but I have prayed for you that your own faith may not fail ... and you (Peter) when ... you have turned back, strengthen your brothers." You seem to expect me to become a rock, Jesus.

And I kept letting you down. How can I strengthen the others, when I can't even help *myself*? When you first called me "Rock," you said you would build your new community on a faith like mine. Some faith! Some rock!

You are dying on a Roman cross and I am hiding — afraid for my life. *You* are the rock, Jesus ... without you I am nothing. *You* are the cornerstone everyone has abandoned. I might have left you long ago too — but you're the only one I've ever known who has the words, the good news, about eternal life. You are the *Lord* ... *my* Lord ... and I need you, Jesus. I need your forgiveness.

Your body is being broken and your blood is being shed — just as you said it would be last night at the supper. Is this the beginning of the new covenant, Jesus? Is there forgiveness for us in your awful death? Is there forgiveness for *me? Please*, let it be so. Forgive me, Jesus ... wash all of me ... change me ... and make me your rock ... for I cannot do it by myself.

At The Empty Tomb:
The Angel

"Hallelujah! Victory!"

Setting
*An angel sits by a cross of Easter lilies or an empty tomb fash-
ioned from boxes or sheets draped over boxes. The resurrection
has already happened and the angel is awaiting the arrival of the
women who would anoint the body of Jesus. The angel reflects on
the events of that early morning, saluting Jesus for his victory and
imagining how Jesus' followers will respond to the resurrection
and its meaning.*

Hallelujah! Hallelujah! *Hallelujah!* It's happened. The tomb is
empty! God the Father has raised his Son to life! What a day of
celebration. What an honor it is to be here. What a victory this is —
for Father God, for Jesus his Son, and for all God's people — and
even us angels. Victory!

Overcome Satan
Yes, you've won. Jesus! You've won. You resisted all of Satan's
tricks and temptations. Out there in the wilderness, the devil wanted
you to doubt your Sonship — to doubt the Father's promise to you.
He even tried to get you to use your power for yourself — to take
an easy way, a way of self-glorification, a way that would have
made Satan Lord. But you said, "No," to him.

But Satan didn't want to take "no" for an answer, did he? After the
transfiguration he was back, speaking through poor Peter, trying to
dissuade you from your calling, tempting you to avoid the cross.
And then in Gethsemane the other night, as the cross loomed larger

and larger. Satan was there again, in the shadows, filling you with dread, trying to drive the Father's love from your mind.

But you always put your trust in your Father, Jesus. Again and again, you remembered your mission, the reason why he sent you into the world. And you trusted him to see you through. You embraced the cross because you trusted your Father's word of promise. What did the Psalmist write?

> *Therefore my heart is glad, and my soul rejoices;*
> *my body also rests secure.*
> *For you do not give me up to Sheol,*
> *or let your faithful one see the Pit.*
> *You show me the path of life.*
> *In your presence there is fullness of joy;*
> *in your right hand are pleasures forevermore.*
>
> — Psalm 16:9-11

Jesus, all of us angels — the whole heavenly host — worship and praise you — for you never doubted your Father or his love for you. You have been everything God intended Adam and Eve to be when he first created them. You have been the Man, *the man of faith and faithfulness*, Adam never was. You have been one with the Father, in your humanity, just as you have always been one with him in your divinity. You are the sinless one, Jesus. And so all of heaven and earth rejoice this day ... for you have overcome Satan and his power to seduce God's people to sin. You've defeated Satan.

Overcome Sin

But you didn't overcome just Satan; no, you've overcome sin, too! And how the world needed to be freed from sin! Humanity has made such a mess of everything. They have turned their backs on God and his love, just as they turned on you this past week; they have cared only about themselves; they have treated each other with indifference, and sometimes with outright contempt. They have sinned and the wages of sin is death. They deserve to die!

46

But you sinned against no one, Jesus. You were without sin. You didn't deserve to die. Yet you willingly gave yourself up to die in their places. You are like the spotless lambs offered in sacrifice for the sins of their owners.

And you did it out of love. You loved these people, just as the Father does. In spite of everything God wants them to love him and to be *his people*. And you loved them just as the Father does — loved them enough to be willing to take their place in death ... to suffer the consequences of their sin, to die their death.

By not giving in to sin and then by embracing the cross, you truly have been God's lamb who has taken away the sins of the world. The Father is pleased with you, Jesus; the whole company of heaven salutes you ... and one day all God's people will thank you and bless you for what you have done for them ... for you have defeated sin and opened the doors to forgiveness.

Overcome Death
And now God has raised you to life, just as he promised. People think that death is the end, Jesus. They think death has the last word, that death is the victor, but God wants them to know that he is making everything new! God is beginning a new creation, a new heaven and a new earth.

Jesus, your resurrection will not be like that of Jairus' daughter, or that of Lazarus. One day they will die. But your resurrection is the beginning of something *new*. You are the first — the first fruits — of those who will rise to live with you forever. Death has been defeated! It is a miracle — the greatest miracle ever!

You have *won*, Jesus! You have overcome all God's enemies, you have set your people free. And this morning, everyone will know it. All creation will celebrate your victory together! Hallelujah!

But right now, your followers are troubled and confused. The disciples are in hiding, the women are even now making plans to come and anoint your body with their tears. They thought you were the long-awaited Messiah and now they think the cross has ended all their hopes. But in the resurrection they will know the truth. They will know that you really *are* the Messiah. God's own beloved son ... *the Victor!*

This morning, the Centurion is having second thoughts. Rome thinks it has succeeded in silencing your gospel. The authorities think that they have solved their problem by killing you. The resurrection will make it clear that no one could have killed God's Son unless he willingly emptied himself, and handed himself over to arrest and execution. The resurrection will make it clear that everything happened according to plan. Everything happened *for them.*

Beloved John can't understand how your dying and God's love fit together. How can your death take away the sin of the world? But when John discovers that you have been raised up, everything will become clear to him and the rest. And he will see that God loved the world so much, that he asked you to come into this world to give your life for this lost creation so that no one would have to perish, but could have *life.*

Simon of Cyrene was so upset and embarrassed for being forced to carry your cross. He couldn't understand how you could forgive your enemies from the cross; he had no idea that your dying meant forgiveness for all who long for it. But the resurrection will help him see that you are the key to forgiveness, life, and salvation.

Peter is still in hiding, still ashamed that he is not the rock he too would like to be. Your resurrection will help him see that today is a new day, that there is hope, that because of you God's people can have a fresh start, a new beginning, they can become "rocks" of faith and faithfulness, just as Peter will become.

And the Marys — your mother, Mary Magdalene, and the rest of the women — they are crushed with grief. But your resurrection will show them that love is never in vain, that their faith was not misplaced, that you will always be there for them, because you are alive forevermore ... even to the end of the age.

Today is a day of victory, my Lord. Sin and death and Satan have been defeated — so let the whole creation shout for joy, for the old has passed away, and the new has begun. Christ is risen! Risen to receive glory and power and might. Risen to receive a name that is above every other name in heaven and on earth — so everyone might know him as we do and call him *Lord*. Hallelujah! Hallelujah! Hallelujah!

Uh oh ... here come the women to anoint Jesus' body. Boy, are *they* in for a surprise.

On The Road:
Two Disciples

"Walking To Emmaus With Jesus"

Setting
Two disciples walk along the road, pausing every so often to talk. Jesus could be among a group following along and listening in with them. Perhaps just before or during the last discussion before Jesus speaks, the figure of Jesus moves from the group closer to the two disciples, and then joins them.

Cleopas: I still can't believe that it's over. Jesus is dead!

Friend: Who would have thought it would come to this?

Cleopas: I know. Jesus seemed to be the answer to all our prayers.

Friend: Remember how he used to come into a room or into a crowd and he made everything okay?

Cleopas: Yes, he would listen to the sick, look at them with the saddest eyes, and then lay his hands on them and make them well.

Friend: And remember the time when the crowds followed him around the lake and it was getting late and everyone was hungry and then Jesus took that boy's loaves and fish and fed all those people?

Cleopas: There must have been thousands there that day.

Friend: Yes ... and then there was the time Jesus met that man full of demons. And Jesus overpowered them and cast all those demons into a herd of pigs and they fell into the lake and drowned!

Cleopas: I never did understand that — but I was sure happy for the man Jesus freed.

Friend: And talk about power! How about the time Jesus and the others were out in their fishing boat and that storm came up and ...

Cleopas: ... and Jesus was asleep, mind you!

Friend: And then he got up and *commanded* the wind and the waves to behave! He had so much power.

Cleopas: Yes. I still don't understand why he didn't use it. I mean, all he had to do was give the word and surely God would have helped him. After all, what they said is true, isn't it? If he could save others, why couldn't he save himself? Or at least he could have asked *us* to help him. I know some of us would have come to his rescue. We were ready to die for him when he entered Jerusalem last week.

Friend: But maybe he thought that wouldn't help. Remember all the things he said to us that never made sense? I mean — *Love your enemies! Forgive those who persecute you!* I don't know if Jesus had the stomach for a good fight. Sure he had strong words for the Pharisees and the Scribes, but Jesus wasn't a fighter.

Cleopas: Maybe you're right. He was kind of tenderhearted. I remember the time the disciples tried to keep all those moms with their babies from bothering Jesus, and as tired as he was he wanted to hold those babies and give them a blessing.

Friend: Maybe Jesus just got tired of all the hassling with the Pharisees and the Scribes.

Cleopas: Maybe when Rome got into the picture, Jesus just gave up. It's easier just to give in than to take on the might of Rome. And what could we accomplish anyway? But it was good while it lasted.

Friend: Yes, it was ... maybe it was just too good to be true ...

(Jesus, following along behind, now steps forward to join these two travelers and begins talking with them.)

Jesus: Good day, friends. Where are you going so late into the afternoon?

Cleopas: We are on our way home, to Emmaus.

Friend: Yes, nothing left in Jerusalem for us, so we're going home.

Jesus: Nothing in Jerusalem? Why, whatever do you mean? Jerusalem is God's city; the Temple is there and the Word is there. And that is where the Messiah is to reign.

Friend: Don't talk to us about the Messiah just now.

Jesus: Why? What's the matter? Aren't you awaiting the Messiah? Perhaps it is this Jesus fellow.

Cleopas: Haven't you heard? Friend, where have you been the past few days?

Jesus: What do you mean?

Cleopas: Well, this Jesus you mentioned has been crucified. It happened last Friday. One of his own disciples betrayed him, handed him over to the religious leaders, and they sent him to Pilate to have him executed.

Jesus: On what charges?

Friend: Blasphemy! They said he claimed to be God's son.

Cleopas: And treason. They said he claimed to be the Messiah and he had plans to overthrow Roman rule.

Friend: But now he is dead.

Cleopas: And we thought that he was the Messiah.

Friend: Yes, we thought he would be the one everyone is waiting for. We thought he would liberate Jerusalem and set the people free.

Jesus: So you don't think this Jesus is the one, eh?

Cleopas: Friend, we don't know what to think. This is the third day since his crucifixion.

Friend: Yes. Jesus is dead.

Cleopas: But this morning some of the women in Jesus' group came into Jerusalem with some wild story that his tomb was empty. All his disciples were alarmed — both by the story and by the women's hysteria. Some of them claimed that they had actually seen angels.

Friend: Yes, they said he was alive! *But after three days?*

Cleopas: So you see, we don't know what to think, or what to believe anymore. We thought Jesus was the one ... but now he's gone and we're afraid of these rumors. We don't want to be disappointed again. I, for one, couldn't take it.

Jesus: Why do you think that the Messiah wouldn't have to suffer? Haven't you heard what Isaiah said about the Messiah? "He was despised and rejected by men, a man of sorrows, and familiar with suffering. Like one from whom men hide their faces he was despised, and we esteemed him not" (Isaiah 53:3 *NIV*).

My friends, the Messiah was bound to suffer because those he came to save would reject him.

Why, the scriptures say that even one of the Messiah's own disciples would betray him. The Psalmist sings for the Messiah and says: "Even my close friend, whom I trusted, he who shared my bread, has lifted up his heel against me" (Psalm 41:9 *NIV*).

Friend: But why would God let this happen? Wouldn't God want the Messiah to prosper and live and to make things better — like Jesus was doing? Wouldn't God want his people to be free of their bondage to Rome?

Jesus: God wants his people to be set free. But Isaiah goes on to say that the Messiah would suffer to set us free but from something much worse than Rome. The Messiah would set us free *from sin.*

The Messiah is like a sacrificial lamb that takes away the sins of God's people. Remember what Isaiah said? "Surely he took up our infirmities and carried our sorrows, yet we considered him stricken by God, smitten by him, and afflicted. But he was pierced for our transgressions, he was crushed for our iniquities; the punishment that brought us peace was upon him, and by his wounds we are healed. We all, like sheep, have gone astray, each of us has turned to his own way; and the Lord has laid on him the iniquity of us all" (Isaiah 53:4-6 *NIV*).

Cleopas: Could it be? Jesus *had* to die? Jesus died for *our* sins? But how do we know that Jesus was the one? How do we know that he was not just another impostor, like all the other would-be Messiahs?

Jesus: Well, think about how he died. He was crucified; and at the foot of the cross the soldiers played dice for his clothes. Remember what the Psalmist said? "Dogs have surrounded me; a band of evil men has encircled me, they have pierced my hands and my feet. I can count all my bones; people stare and gloat over me. They divide my garments among them and cast lots for my clothing" (Psalm 22:16-18 *NIV*).

The Psalmist was showing us what the Messiah would experience. And remember how quickly Jesus died? Why, the soldiers didn't have to break his legs to speed up the process. Jesus died just like a sacrificial lamb slain for Passover. God told the people that "they must not leave any of it till morning or break any of its bones" (Numbers 9:12 *NIV*).

Friend: Yes, but the Romans are crucifying a lot of people these days. There are plenty of would-be Messiahs. How do we know that Jesus is any different? And if he did die for our sins, how do we know that it worked, that Jesus' dying could have taken away our sins?

Jesus: Well, you yourselves have told me of the women's report — how the tomb was empty this morning and how some of them said they had seen angels who said this Jesus is alive. Why should it surprise you that God would not let his Son remain among the dead? The Psalmist said, "Therefore my heart is glad and my tongue rejoices; my body also will rest secure, because you will not abandon me to the grave, nor will you let your Holy One see decay. You have made known to me the path of life; you will fill me with joy in your presence, with eternal pleasures at your right hand" (Psalm 16:9-11 *NIV*).

No one should be surprised that God would raise his Son to life. Didn't Jesus tell the disciples the same thing? That the Son of Man must suffer many things, and then on the third day be raised again?

Cleopas: Could it be?

(They walk on a little bit, the two friends pondering all this. Cleopas is surprised by how fast the trip has gone.)

Cleopas: Here we are already! Welcome to our village and to our house.

Jesus: Yes, but I must be going on. So much to do and so little time.

Friend: Yes, but, "stay with us, for it is nearly evening; the day is almost over."

Cleopas: Yes, stay with us. You must be as famished as we are and a good night's rest will give you new life for the morning.

Friend: Yes, there is so much to talk about yet. You must be a rabbi yourself. Listening to you on the road has helped to open my eyes a bit. Why, before I was so down and now I can't wait to tell the others what we've learned. So please stay. We'll just get something simple to eat and in the morning we will have a feast.

Jesus: Well, if you really want me to. I would be honored to be your guest and a part of your family.

Friend: Good! Here, take the place of honor at our table. I'll be right back.

(All of them go into the "house" area. When the bread and wine are brought in, they are placed in front of Jesus. The other two sit down with Jesus. Jesus takes the bread, gives thanks.)

Jesus: Praised are you, O Lord our God, our Father, ruler of the Universe, for endless is your mercy and eternal your reign. You have filled all creation with light and life; heaven and earth are full of your glory.

Through Abraham and Sarah you promised to bless all nations. In power and great glory you rescued Israel your chosen from the oppression of Pharaoh; you shielded your people from the angel of death; delivered them out of the hands of their pursuers and, by fire and cloud, led them through the sea out of despair and slavery into freedom and the land you had promised.

Through the prophets you renewed your promise; and, at this the end of all the ages, you sent your Son, who in words and deeds proclaimed your kingdom and was obedient to your will, even to giving his life.[1]

Praised are you, O Lord our God, our Father, ruler of the Universe, who brings forth bread from the earth.

Take and eat, this is my body.

(At this point, Cleopas and Friend scratch their heads, look at each other, and get up from the table, move to the front of it to talk about what's been going on. As they talk, Jesus exits behind them.)

Cleopas: Could it be? Could he be Jesus? But how could it be? How could we have talked with him on the road all the way home and not recognized him?

Friend: I don't know, but it *has* to be him! Didn't your heart warm inside you when he talked about the Messiah and pointed out all the scriptures to us along the way?

Cleopas: Yes, that's true. It seems as if Jesus himself were talking with us through those passages.

Friend: Well, *he was!* And *he's right here with us now*, sharing a meal with us!

(Here the two friends turn around to the table and discover that Jesus has vanished. Overwhelmed, they decide to go back to Jerusalem to tell the others that they have seen the Lord.)

Friend: What happened to him? Where'd he go?

Cleopas: Quickly ... let's get out of here. We've got to tell the others. We've seen the Lord. He is alive!

Friend: He really is alive!

Cleopas: And to think we didn't recognize him until we met him in the bread he broke and the word he spoke.

Friend: Yes! Let's go. Hallelujah!

(Both exit with "Hallelujahs" on their lips.)

---

1. Quoted and adapted from a eucharistic prayer in *Lutheran Book of Worship* (Minneapolis: Augsburg Publishing House, 1978), p. 69.

CPSIA information can be obtained
at www.ICGtesting.com
Printed in the USA
LVHW081051270120
644900LV00016B/664